'Like being tickled whilst watching an Al[...] accessible comedic strokes painted w[...] backdrop often tinged with pathos an[...] poems sit like relics to bumbling humanity in a well-loved museum. A truly brilliant collection.'

CLARE FERGUSON-WALKER

'A collection of often funny, often romantic and always fascinating verse'

BOYD CLACK

'These poems take the everyday – park benches, libraries, caravans – and transform them, through sharp wit and blithe observation, into something far more quirky. Easygoing and candid, their humour is balanced by a fine sense of pathos: indeed, there often lies, in these familiar things, the shadow of their loss.

Liveliness and humour are laced with melancholy or yearning, creating poems which are well-rounded, engaging, and full of surprise. Expressed in Blayney's inimical and unique style, these are poems for the everyday, and for everyone. A brilliant collection indeed.'

MAB JONES

'The line between page and performance has flummoxed and exhilarated poets for generations. This collection finds Mark Blayney stepping into the spotlight, not just to read or to write on that line but to dance on it, tell jokes on it, ride unicycles on it.

'This wonderful collection of accessible, witty, original and brilliantly-imagined poems reflects on the quirks and magic of living in the 21st century. A man falls in love with a statue he spots in Italy. Saturday's football results are re-imagined in a way that will never let you hear them in quite the same way again. A pair of long-distance trucks becomes a hilarious metaphor for a relationship.

'This collection made me laugh more than any has done for a long time. Its lasting gift is to allow us to see our everyday lives in startlingly new ways, and the collection is so generous and welcoming to readers that this is a gift Blayney gives, with a wink, to us all.'

JONATHAN EDWARDS

'Full of verve, wit and incredibly funny. These poems shine like floodlights at a match or sometimes there is just a twinkle in the eye of the page that catches your attention and gives you a knowing wink. He ain't stupid this man, he can make football scores out of Shakespeare, his love poems are poignant and the images he conjures up hang around in your head like ghosts. I love this book, I'm giving it to everybody for Christmas, birthdays, bar mitzvahs…'

IFOR THOMAS

Loud music makes
you drive faster

Mark Blayney won the Somerset Maugham Prize for *Two Kinds of Silence*. His second book *Conversations with Magic Stones* was described by John Bayley as 'remarkable... as good as some of the best of Elizabeth Bowen' and his third book *Doppelgangers* is also published by Parthian.

A regular performance poet and MC, Mark's been longlisted for the National Poetry Competition, is a National Poetry Slam finalist and a John Tripp Award for Spoken Poetry finalist.

He's the world's first *ABBA Life Coach*, in which he uses the Power of the 70s to help you achieve love, happiness and wear more spandex, and is also the world's first fully accredited *Professor of Boney M Studies*. He'll be presenting these shows at a theatre or festival near you soon (depending on where you live).

www.markblayney.weebly.com

Loud music makes you drive faster

Mark Blayney

PARTHIAN

Parthian, Cardigan SA43 1ED
www.parthianbooks.com
First published in 2016
© Mark Blayney 2016
ISBN 978-1910901793
Editor: Susie Wild
Cover design by Torben Schacht
Typeset by Elaine Sharples
Printed in EU by Pulsio SARL
Published with the financial support of the Welsh Books Council
British Library Cataloguing in Publication Data
A cataloguing record for this book is available from the British Library.

Contents

umbers

...d me of you

...of your breasts
...as you turn on one leg
...the bath

...of your knee
...as you bend to kiss me

...re
...rl from *Countdown*

Blue Trouser Blues

You left your jeans on the radiator
and I woke later and saw half of you
drying by the wall.

I move you to the window
where it's sunnier and you'll dry quicker.
The next day you're crisp and sharp

and can stand on the carpet.
To give you body I fill your legs
with plastic bags hoarded

so when I go shopping I can save the planet.
I never remember though. They're more use
giving the half of you ballast.

It's hard to get your figure right
and I can see you removing some,
twisting round and saying

do my plastic bags look big in this?
You walk halfly across my floor now.
I find some shoes that fit

and go to see you, depositing you
on the path. You're out, it seems.
I leave you mid-stride to wait

and later, dream that half of you
walks carefully, decisively through the snow,
bringing the rest of you with her.

Florence

I want to marry
  that statue we saw in Italy;
    it was the glance she gave me
      when the guards weren't looking.

    Age will not weary her –
well she's already a hundred but
looking pretty good on it.

    And when I'm an old man,
      she'll gaze on me with the same expression
        although at that stage I will probably say,
          'Please put on some clothes.'

      If you're reading this now,
        I'm sorry I haven't been in touch.
      I've been meaning to write:
actually, I did call twice but
  the museum wouldn't put me through;
  in fact they hung up on me.

    I found a photo of her online,
    keep it in my wallet,
    cement her picture
     into the walls

     and at the party,
     the house buzzing with energy,
   the guests all wonder
why my wife's expression is somewhat
stony-faced.

Forgetting your Birthday

I'm just not good with dates
names, places
remembering where I've put things
what time we said we'd meet
this is all part of my charm
I do think about you a lot
and it's the thought that counts.

I will buy a diary
if I remember
and fill it with birthdays
in the meantime
why not move in?
You could set my clocks for me
you can forgive me
to your heart's content
I do love you, Milly
Melanie, sorry.

I am improving
my alarm clock is on timer
this morning I accidentally
pulled the plug out
can we meet this evening
and re-set things
before…

I always feel that I'm forgetting
something vital
what is it that I need to remember
before… before…
what is it. Tell me. Surely someone
will tell us
before it's too late.

Blue Trouser Blues

You left your jeans on the radiator
and I woke later and saw half of you
drying by the wall.

I move you to the window
where it's sunnier and you'll dry quicker.
The next day you're crisp and sharp

and can stand on the carpet.
To give you body I fill your legs
with plastic bags hoarded

so when I go shopping I can save the planet.
I never remember though. They're more use
giving the half of you ballast.

It's hard to get your figure right
and I can see you removing some,
twisting round and saying

do my plastic bags look big in this?
You walk halfly across my floor now.
I find some shoes that fit

and go to see you, depositing you
on the path. You're out, it seems.
I leave you mid-stride to wait

and later, dream that half of you
walks carefully, decisively through the snow,
bringing the rest of you with her.

Florence

I want to marry
   that statue we saw in Italy;
     it was the glance she gave me
       when the guards weren't looking.

   Age will not weary her –
well she's already a hundred but
looking pretty good on it.

   And when I'm an old man,
      she'll gaze on me with the same expression
        although at that stage I will probably say,
        'Please put on some clothes.'

      If you're reading this now,
       I'm sorry I haven't been in touch.
     I've been meaning to write:
     actually, I did call twice but
     the museum wouldn't put me through;
     in fact they hung up on me.

  I found a photo of her online,
   keep it in my wallet,
   cement her picture
    into the walls

   and at the party,
    the house buzzing with energy,
the guests all wonder
why my wife's expression is somewhat
stony-faced.

Forgetting your Birthday

I'm just not good with dates
names, places
remembering where I've put things
what time we said we'd meet
this is all part of my charm
I do think about you a lot
and it's the thought that counts.

I will buy a diary
if I remember
and fill it with birthdays
in the meantime
why not move in?
You could set my clocks for me
you can forgive me
to your heart's content
I do love you, Milly
Melanie, sorry.

I am improving
my alarm clock is on timer
this morning I accidentally
pulled the plug out
can we meet this evening
and re-set things
before…

I always feel that I'm forgetting
something vital
what is it that I need to remember
before… before…
what is it. Tell me. Surely someone
will tell us
before it's too late.

the numbers
remind me of you

the 3 of your breasts
the 4 as you turn on one leg
to run the bath

the 7 of your knee
the 9 as you bend to kiss me

you are
the girl from *Countdown*

Football Results

Gok Wan
　　　　Everton nil

Birmingham six
　　　　Guildford four

Channel five
　　　　Mouth of, seven

Tenerife 95
　　　　Iceland £1.99

Motherwell, thanks for asking
　　　　Figure of, eight

Real Madrid three,
　　　　Unreal Madrid, banana

Heaven 17
　　　Haircut 100

You, two
　　　Me, late thirties

Your call 0898
　　　　My call, Jackson

Fast Forward

my mum's neighbour
is a hundred and six

we go next door
for her birthday party

drinks too much sherry
the minx

her memory's failing
she tells me

with a twinkle in her eye that there's something
she's supposed to have done

but can't remember
for the life of her what it is

it can't be important I say
oh no she replies, of course not

I like this idea
of ignoring the details

to the extent that
they don't happen

fast forward a year
next week she's 107

she wants to go to Alton Towers
we all agree, it'll be heaven

Trucks

Parallel on the motorway
like lovers, one inches ahead of the other

flirtatiously, the first
flashes his lights

the second, let's call him Bruno
moves slowly in front, positioning his bulk

ready for the first, we'll call him Mitch,
to nestle up behind

they look rather like each other
Mitch is a little longer, and Bruno

has a cheeky curve to his roof
his slope bouncing rhythmically

as we go over chevrons.
They stay together past Stafford and Chester

though going uphill, Bruno wearies.
The middle is tough, it's true

and all relationships are compromise.
We think back to the M5, when all was easy

and watch a white van scoot past,
zipping in without signalling.

Bruno and Mitch delicately ignore
the crude filth he displays

the fingered *Actually, my wife is this dirty*
on his greying back.

Chugging clouds of exhaustion,
Mitch turns off before the border.

I'm surprised; I thought they'd go
off into the sunset together.

Anyway, as we forgo England Bruno forges
his lonely path for a few more miles until

an Eddie Stobart truck falls in line behind
and the game starts again.

What a tart! I hope Eddie realises
what an old roué Bruno is.

Still, I observe as I accelerate past,
men just like trucking. I give Bruno a friendly wave,

a wink and try to do that arm gesture
though it's difficult when you're behind a wheel

and want him to see you in the mirror.
Bruno, absently scratching stubble

looks at me as if I'm mental.
I don't know why. Perhaps my tail light is out.

I reach the port and watch
the black box silhouettes.

We're anonymous here, the trucks lie by
each other like toughened floozies;

it's intimate, but don't expect any kisses.
The sea and Shetland glitter in the distance

and I think back to the Lizard. This journey
and its mythological status haunts me

but my friendly truckers,
burgers passed through the window

keep me grounded. When they are asleep
talismen in the window dance in the breeze

and watch the wheels. When the trucks are moving
the trinkets are still

but now, motionless against the concrete
we watch them speed, speed, speed.

Winning Wager

Playing chess
you stripped to distract me
illegal move

for a bet
we went to the shops
wearing our long coats
and nothing else

who won the money?
Tesco.

On not going on holiday

The brochure promises
autumn sun
I turn the leaves

There's a palm tree
waving at me from the beach

There are one hundred and fourteen resorts
each with the same swimming pool

I lose myself
inside the glossy pages
that smell of an exotic, tropical
printing factory

On Rewriting

the first draft of anything is shit
ernest hemingway wrote

in the afternoon he revised it
shit might cause offence
he changed it to rubbish

the first draft of anything is rubbish
in the evening over whisky
he saw this was rubbish

he changed it back to shit
the first draft of anything is shit
right let's go hunt some leopards

On Standing Next to Harold Pinter

There was so much to say
      plays stories poems wars –

but standing next to Harold Pinter
in the Royal Court Theatre
      toilet,

none of it seemed appropriate,
      apart
      from

      the

long

pause.

Roath Park

Our son destroys flowers.
He does it with such love – bringing me the pieces –
that I'm sure Dennis and Elsie,
whose bronzed names burnish the toddler-climbed bench,
won't mind.
Petals are laid in front of them.

We walk slowly, wobbily, through the ha-ha.
He even says it as he goes. Ha ha!
We have spawned a genius.
Well, that's what every parent says.
And they're right.

Library

High ceilings. I felt reserved.
There's a plaque to someone
I should have heard of.
Risking displeasure
o'er chasm of counter
when I was a boy
I asked for a *Dandy*.
We don't have that here, young man.

Well, things have changed.
These days it's lime green.
As I push-pull the pram
there's a closure-fearing welcome
that borders hysteria.
And I find it's me that's thinking,
can't he take that call outside?
And, why are they stocking this rubbish?
And that, why, that's practically porn!

I get my son his card. Fourteen
books he can take out, and he's not yet 1.
Ex-libris we lie on the grass and look above
Victorian twiddly bits to a flat, Deco sky.
Planes mondrian what seem random lines
yet we know they're preciser than clockwork.
Together, we read the first
of your fourteen books.
Bob the Builder.
Reflective looks.

Haiku Day

Eating

I knew you'd be sweet
when I saw your address
was on Quality Street.

Drinking

Teetotal for a year.
Really it was a week.
Just felt like a year.

Reading

We've been reading Dickens
for two hundred years.
That's why they seem so long.

Cleaning

I looked hard
for the Vanish this morning.
Couldn't find it anywhere.

The Sticks

Paddington steps where
pedestrians behave like cars:

here is a man who
eats an apple in three bites.

Face on the bridge like my gran,
thinking, *What's he looking at?*

not really knowing where I'm going
(or when).

She, city-trained,
steps through cars like Frogger,

a grin as I try to keep up,
her house confirming

we've left the present.
The Georgian doorway a sci-fi portal.

I help her
with the skillet and Aga

on grapes and cheese we remember
how speedy and sexy uni was and

the brief time we were together
seeming an age. Neither of us

sees anyone any more
and one of our number is dead.

She talks of the house
as a master who lets her out

to work, day unto day
leasing her body while it serves

its purpose. Of course, we went to bed;
it would have seemed impolite

of one or other of us not to
but there was a longing for something,

and I plan to go but you offer me deodorant
and so, Regent's Park, post coitus

a stark hot mayday, time conflating
as I return through the portal and

on a boat, the violent indigo not telling us
what we might not be thinking

Travelling Round Britain

Start Point. Steppingley. Sticklepath. Claudy. Thundersley. Wetwang. Bicker. Blubberhouses.

Idle. Beer. Rum. Downham. Slaughter. Little Snoring. Great Snoring. Crawley. Sicklington.

Rock. Wham. Kilkenny. Skull. Bury. Runwell.

Hasland. Privett. Bushey. Trowell. Trim. Sheering. Maze. Neatishead. Lovet.

Three cocks. Blackrod. Woodrising. Knocklong. Cummer.

Ham. Egg. Curry. Cookham. Burnham. Eatwell. Hartburn. Six Mile Bottom. Walkden.

Plymouth Hoe. Singleton. Shirley. Leggs. Rear. Ampleforth. Feltham. Staines.

Saintbury. Tresco. Spa. Asdee. Debenham. Sale.

Tory Island. Ladybank. Moneygall. Longhope. Miserden. Faccombe.

Totland. Playden. Childwall. Watchet. Falfield. Stargazey.

Faceby. Swineshead. Twatt. Punchbowl. Swords. Pollokshields.

Lover. Penn. Letterfinish. Ifold. Seal. Box. Starcross. Lustleigh. Bride. Honeybourne.

Performing a Poem in a Non-poetry Space

Hello, my name is *Cough*.
I'd like to share my *what the hell's this?* with you
and also to welcome *bar till ping*.
It's lovely to see *excuse me love* here and also
so many of you who are *mower starts outside window*.

SO I'LL SPEAK a little louder to cover the *Is this not Cuban salsa?*
and hopefully we can move to the first *well they told me it was in here*
and then we'll enjoy a reading from a new book by
oh you're right it's Thursday.

It's good to see so many new faces *FART*
and I hope not all of our first-time performers will be nervous.

So *don't listen to him it's all indoctrination,*
put your bible away you wan- kingdom of the polar bear,
a set of poems about Greenland and the
ice sheet – *me, let's put something on the jukebox!*

And please welcome to the stage, reading from her new book
'Poems Spoken in a Whisper'
the very wonderful *Police siren! Bar till! Where are the toilets?*
 Good evening. My first poem is called, 'The Long Silence'.

...

...

...

Let's go, Doris. We're missing Casualty.

Poem for John Cooper Clarke

I met my wife on a number 9 bus
I was instantly consumed with claustrophobic lust
She said *this feels like an all-time mare*
I said *would you like to continue this discussion upstairs*
Ten minutes on top of an ageing Routemaster
We talked and laughed and at a red light, the bus went faster
We dwelled in the light of a topless carriage
It was twelve steps up and a short-lived marriage
We had one child and wanted sex

To be love-filled and meaningful; I said *have you met my ex?*
She liked kids too, I should have heeded the warning
She said *I want to have your children*;
I said *I'll bring them round in the morning*.

I broke my neck, they gave me one of them collars
That they put on dogs when they've spent all your dollars
On cuffing and fighting and shitting on all fours
It keeps you focused but you can't lick your balls
It's no life really for a self-respecting dog
Like being on page three for an existential god:
You can get your tits out, but no one will believe it
And if they do they won't think they've actually seen it.
It's self-referential poetry, it leaves us all in the dark
So if you don't like it, don't watch John Cooper Clarke.

Late Night Last Night

one small step for man
one giant leap for mankind
oh… that's the same thing.
why's no one noticed?
sorry. I should have said,
one small step for <u>a</u> man,
one giant leap for mankind.
can we…
can we go again?

Neil's Wife Replies

one small step for a person
one giant leap for humankind
you see Neil if you'd made it less sexist
you wouldn't have stumbled
although it's true that
it doesn't have quite the same
rhetorical power.
bollocks.

Static Caravan

it doesn't go anywhere

it has wheels
it doesn't go anywhere

it has a tow bar
it's cemented to the ground

it can travel the world
but it looks at the same bit of sea
every day

it's an attractive bit of sea
there's a nice tree as well

but its soul pines
for movement

in its dreams
it grows wings
rips itself from the concrete
and flies, like an ungainly, portly version
of Chitty Chitty Bang Bang

across the desert
across the seas

singing, 'I am a static caravan

on holiday!'

Severn Bridge

Driving Wales to England
there's a windsock so you know
what the breeze is like.

Why isn't there one
on the other side?
In a way I'm pleased

that, like me,
even a giant bridge
can lose its socks.

More embarrassing for the bridge
because its ones are bright orange and huge –
I can imagine its mum, saying 'For goodness sake
how can you lose that?'

West of the bridge
we drive through stunning earth –

bracken on mountains,
ice blue lakes freeze,
soil compressed by blackened sky –

scanning the horizon for a glimpse
of the gigantic sofa
that the sock might be behind.

The Book of Truth

Salman Rushdie
has got into trouble again
for writing about the obesity epidemic
endemic in our kids.

Some irate parents have declared

a fat war on him.

8am Grafton Street

Waitress monochrome
I try to be human

is everything all right for you there?

yes but what made it better
stirring the coffee was resting my
head on your leg

the rise and sway
of the lake of your stomach
beetroot stains on your hands and

you pause for an answer then walk
a little too quickly away

coffee machine grinding to itself

who does he –

view from your window flat roofs
diagonal of green you wind your hair
in my finger

later the meeting
the job evaporates with
a sentence how quickly
the dull and mundane ruptures

then is looked back on fondly
I long for the boredom yes

machine grumbling fiercely now
I eat the small biscuit

you blur to the kitchen

we tip crumbs from the sheets
your night table a stack of art books
I like it here you whisper
lying on your front *yes*   gurgles

the machine is exhausted

you glance an eyebrow
will he ever leave?

yes   I pay the bill
newspaper umbrella I am the picture
of the office worker
though not beyond today

your automatic smile as I go

shows a flicker in your eye as you recall
our long afternooned morning

Homeward

Another day fishing
Mum rolling her eyes
I don't know why he bothers
he never catches anything

triumphant hunter
padding up the drive
trophy from bulging bicep
mum's arms folding

we *don't even like fish anyway*
I suppose we'll have to bake it
she lays down newspaper
the guts – *the mess* she tuts

it fights and wrestles him
despite being dead
Dad mutters at it, calls it
bastard we sit in a crown

at the table, not knowing
how long this will take
the smell
was of forgotten swimming costumes

blood pooled about the head
Dad wielded, for our benefit, then dropped
a fat knife which embedded in his leg
he brushed off Mum's eruption *chrissake*

but the pouring would not stop
fish, bored, stared eyelessly
at the kitchen strip light as the nurse
struggled to coax Dad

towards a vivid blue
the fish needs cooking *before it goes off*
and stinks out the we wrap him gently in foil
place him on the oven tray and wait fifty minutes,
fifty more, then fifty more.

sequence

my klimt model
  red hair
    patchwork of sins

stockings
  wet in april rain
    silver birch

salted mussels
  licking fingers
    organs dancing

our summer over
  consolation
    autumn calm

october wasp
  drunk on cider
    buttersquash

december sun
  final romance
    blossoming

pregnant with you
  I wonder
    when we will meet

Last commute

The 08:20 winds out slowly.
A child standing on a wall waves.

When my carriage draws parallel I wave back.
The boy jumps up, tugs dad's arm

points at me – he waved!
The train pulls into town;

the alien dome of Paddington.
At the jaw of the Underground

I pause by the entrance, its opening ominous.
In front of Costa Coffee

I wave at the milling people
criss-crossing ahead.

I will go to work
when someone waves back.

Protest march *6 February 2016*

There's an eagle
      on the roof of City Hall

      the more I look up
the more I feel I'll fall.

Ode to Captain Cook

I went to get a lousy t-shirt
and all I came back with
was Australia

Shakespearian football results

Richard 3	Henry 4
Malcolm 1	Macbeth 0
Love's Labour's LOST	Don JUAN
Romey ~ 0	Julie ~ 8
Gentlemen of Verona, 2	Noble Kinsmen, 2
Night 12	Othell 0

Much ado about 0.   Comedy of Errors: 6
I mean, 5.
No, actually, it was 3.

Fortinbras 1   Denmark 0
~ Rosencrantz and Guildenstern were sent off ~

Sonnet 14   Ophelia Nun

Black swan

I I
was was
alarmed alarmed
to to
find find
that that
not not
only only
is is
a a
black black
swan swan
an an
unexpected unexpected
event event

but but
that that
in in
Roath Roath
Park Park
in in
Cardiff Cardiff
we we
have have
two two
of of
them them

who who
saw saw

that that
coming coming

question question
mark mark

to to
get get
over over
this this
surprise surprise
we we
eat eat
couscous

What I Learnt from ABBA

At Waterloo, Napoleon did not surrender.

What actually happened was that Blucher and Wellington
in the Seventh Coalition drove the French from the field
in a classic pincer movement breaking the right flank.

It was much much later that the Allies entered France
from the United Kingdom of the Netherlands
or what is now modern-day Belgium
and restored Louis XVIII to the throne.

Only then did Napoleon abdicate
and face exile on St Helena
where he was heard to admit, 'I tried
to hold you back, but you were stronger.
Oh yeah. And now it seems my only chance
is giving up the fight.' At which point
according to Wellington's biographer
the Duke riposted that the history book
on the shelf is always repeating itself.

Not wanting to be outdone, Napoleon
had the final word, shortly before
he died in 1821, saying, 'How
could I ever refuse? I feel like I win,
when I lose.' He then, according to observers,
sighed his final sigh.

My my. At Waterloo, Napoleon did not surrender.

Lionel Richie Songs that Didn't Chart

'You're Once, Twice, Seventeen Times My Dyslexic Girlfriend'

'I'm Hard Work, Like Monday Morning'

and of course the all-time classic

'Hello? Is it Me You're Looking For? No? Sod You Then.'

This Week in Bee Gee News

More than a woman –
a song about a young lady the Bee Gees met while on holiday in Thailand.

Tragedy –
when your great song is covered by a lesser band, *it's tragedy.*

Words –
it's been alleged that words are all we have to take another person's heart away. This is bad dating advice. There are many things one has access to that can take a person's heart away. Flowers, chocolates, a BMW 3 series, etc. In fact, if words really are all you have to take a person's heart away, you may well find yourself on a hiding to nothing, ending up with no person's heart at all. *Ooh yeah.*

You win again –
but if the other person is always winning, we have to ask: is it something we're doing wrong, or does our negative thinking need addressing?

You should be dancing –
although when another band imitates your sound, voice and style then concludes they *don't feel like dancing*, what can you do?

Morrissey cheers up

Oh, everyday is like payday

    Oh, maybe just one chicken nugget

        Oh, girlfriend in a coma
        (but she might get better)

Hotel, Turin

in a crumpled shirt
the shape of a naked woman

that night I mould it the same way
sleep next to her

morning, she's gone before I wake
my arm resting on the clothes she left behind

keeping her linen scent
the ghost remains as I stalk the room

moon a scythe / home too soon
shirt, wardrobe, breeze

Poem Written Backwards

Cuff
Cuff
Cuff

Then it cuff.
You love still I
Me than looking better he's okay
You for more do couldn't I
Low pretty is text by dumping!
Again try we can?

Then you cuff
Cuff
Cuff
Cuff
It
Cuff

Title.

Waterloo Gardens

So we're famous now –
they closed the street
to film *Doctor Who*.

Yellow signs blocking each end
and on the day
we peered through windows

to see who would invade.
A shame, I remember thinking,
that none of us has children –

they'd love to see this.
I sat by the cat flap and called Sally
across the road

(they told us
we couldn't come out of
our front doors).

She wanted to see Daleks
(or even Cybermen) but there was nothing:
just some people with baseball caps

and trucks like mutant
ice cream vans
and giant lights

like mushroom bulbs.
After all the excitement
we felt a bit short-changed

– nothing to see –
and I washed up and wondered
if I'd missed something.

Á la Proust

so I thought I couldn't remember
anything about school

and then the smell of crayons
brought it all back, somewhat colourfully

the day I pushed Peter Muhler down the slide
and he broke his toe

the time I tried to kiss Natasha Bliss
and she told the teacher

the day Mr Fisk chased me round the classroom
with a wooden metre ruler and it broke on my back

he wasn't very impressed when all his broken rulers
got replaced with bendy plastic ones

that time we took our clothes off
and were found on the playing fields; all this

has led me to some telling conclusions
á la Proust, to stop smelling crayons

After Magritte

If He exists, he's like one of those adverts for Silk Cut.
Beautiful. Obscure.
That bit of purple cloth, with something magical
alluded to behind.
And the nagging doubt that it's all smoke and mirrors.
Still, lots of people like it, and it doesn't seem to do them any harm.

These days, folk get cross. They don't want it in their magazines.
You have to go and smoke in a corner, out of sight.
One day, there'll hardly be any smokers left
and people will find it hard to believe
that anyone ever did smoke, knowing what we know now.
Then we'll miss them.

Some Newly-discovered Extracts from the Diary of Philip Larkin

Dec 8
John Lennon got shot today.
He once sang, 'all you need is love'.
He was wrong.
What he should have sung was,
'all you need is love
plus a bullet-proof cardigan'.

Dec 24
There are 80 Christmases.
Each one
less Christmassy than the last.

Jan 19
I see the new library
and I want to paint it black.

Feb 3
If at first you don't succeed, what did you expect?

Mar 9
Have decided to change my life, as have realised that I need to
    be happier.
Walked through the cemetery wondering how to achieve this.
A dead bird under a tree gave me no clues.
At home recognised that the way to be happy is to take an
    interest in modern music.
Here comes the sun.
But it always goes away again.

Apr 16

I was going to go on holiday, and then I discovered there's no point.

It's just the same as here, except it's too hot to read.

May 9

Have focused more on this idea of enjoying popular music.

Feel, if I may be so bold, that I have rather got the hang of it, because I have got the moves like Jagger.

Like Jagger.

Like Jagger, Jagger.

Jagger; Jagger; Jagger.

July 9

Jagger.

Hi-fi

Winter sun
lies low
in open doorways

Our relationship now
the tune the record plays
when it reaches the label

The Ballad of David Dimbleby

This is a song for David Dimbleby
He's the brother, he's the brother
Of Jonathan Dimbleby

What is the question, time for guests to disagree
That is the question, to dimbleby or not to dimbleby

So the next time you see him, high five to Dimbleby
He'd like to commentate on that, if he's not too busy
With presentating duties on the royal family
What fun for you and me, he's worth his salary,

He's the man of the day

…vid Dimbleby
And we all willingly pay
For the jubilee
jubilee, jubilee,
Dimbleby. Join us next time
in Swansea.

Winning Poem

Lucian Freud
pausing in losing thousands at races
bought a horse and called it Gorn Myson
so that commentators describing its path
alongside pedigree champions had to shout

Gorn Myson, Gorn Myson and thus
will it to victory.

                     As Freud's grandfather
might have told him, *no cigar.*

This didn't bother Lucian
as he bled endless fortunes and foaled
the world's most beautiful paintings.

Platform 4

I Am Sorry To Announce
That The 19: 52 Service From Cardiff Central
Has Been Delayed By Approximately
Eight
Een
Minutes. I Am Very Sorry For This Inconvenience.

What's Worse Is That I Am Not Even
A Real Human Being. That Can Take
Some Getting Used To I Can Tell You.
You Think You've Got Problems
With Your Train Running
Eight
Een
Minutes Late. Think Of How Bad Things Are
For Me.

And Remember
It's Better To Travel
Than It Is
To Arriva.

Ex communication

there was an image of you
on my toast this morning

I covered you in marmalade
and licked it all off

for lunch I had an apple
its pips your initial

afternoon walk
a cloud like your shoulder

over dinner the chair opposite
reflects wine that we spilled

the washing up gurgles
muttering get over her, get over her

oh I have, I say blithely
to your ghost on the sofa

It's Not a Competition

you said with your
winning smile

your hair cast across your breast
the long illuminated tail
warning of danger

we both cheated at snap
the card trick
of your heart on your sleeve

we split
when you said you weren't interested
in playing games

Tunisia

I was in that hotel. I walked on that beach.
I lazed under those coconut umbrellas
that blurred on the mobile footage.
I ate fruit from a tray, I was served alcohol.
I took pictures, I flew home. A year later
I watched the news today, oh boy.
I didn't write a song. I didn't write a poem.
I didn't do anything.
I hoped, because there's a little bit of hope left.
You can trim layers of hope, like skin from a thumb.
Usually, it grows back.

Butterfly

fragile
means needing to be
agile

Hard to Say

Scalextric. Scalextric. Scalextric.
We furrow the plastic road
fearful of the grinding moment
that spins us off to nowhere.
Those who are left ignore us,
fingers sweaty from the trigger,
speeding up then slowing down,
living their lives. Doing it
right. Getting somewhere.

You Say I Talk Too Much

You
Say
I
Talk
Too
Much

I
Don't
Think
That's
True

Although
On
The
Other
Hand
It
Might
Be

I
Love
You
But
I
Cannot
Get
A
Word
In
Edgew—

Freeku of the City

Orange mist
blur of headlights
club closing

Passed-out girl
skirt high
moon setting

Six am Saturday
taxi and drag queen
pirouetting

Three Very Very Short Shorts

Living in Wales
I am a legal immigrant!
But I still have to pay
£6.50 every time I want to come in.

What To Do
Smash the state!
Abolish capitalism!
Come up with a workable alternative.

Oh You Pretty Thing!
Nothing rhymes with David Bowie.
Now you're gone, we're feeling lowie.
We want you back, to say hello-y.

Serendipity

The heart is a harsh lawyer,
its chambers
beating darkly,
working long hours,
the office messy around it –
no one seemingly doing any work.

That night we were robbed of an hour,
the clocks wrong in the morning,
telling us lazily
it was still winter.

And that's how I met you
on the wrong train
seeing, from rackety Devon tracks,
an ocean outside
curving at the corners
in disbelief.

Love

It's your look that's held me.
The expression Vermeer.
The feeling, silk.

I am going

I am going to start burning bridges
because N Power is so expensive these days.

I am going to begin the begin.
What else can you do with it?

I am going to go back in time and kill Hitler.
I'm not doing anything Thursday, and neither is he.

I am going to put up a blue plaque to commemorate
the place where the blue plaque scheme was thought up

I am going to enjoy myself, once I have sorted out
some crap that will use the day up.

I am going to leave the stage—

The Font of All Knowledge

Today

I

FEEL

Like

Wearing

A

New

Face

Acknowledgements

The Interpreter's House, Spilling Cocoa Over Martin Amis, BBC The One Show, The Delinquent, Buzz, The Merry Maker, East Midlands Young Writers Award, Iain Rennie *Rhyme and Reason* anthology, *Made in Roath: Volume 1, Rhyme and Real Ale Anthology.*

New Poetry from Parthian

Featuring poets from Wales and across Europe,
Parthian Poetry presents:

The Elephant's Foot
by M. A. Oliver-Semenov

Love What is Mortal
by Norman Schwenk

Loud music makes you drive faster…
by Mark Blayney

Cawl
by Siôn Tomos Owen

And Suddenly You Find Yourself
by Natalie Ann Holborow

Tattoo on Crow Street
by Kate Noakes

Washing My Hair With Nettles
by Emilia Ivancu (Translated from Romanian)

A Butterfly's Tremblings in the Digital Age
by Eleni Cay (Translated from Slovakian)

Living in the Delta: New and Collected Poems
by Landeg White

parthianbooks.com